QUILT BLOCKS
go wild!

by Eleanor Levie
& Celebrity Quilters

LEISURE ARTS
the art of everyday living
www.leisurearts.com

LEISURE ARTS, INC.
Little Rock, Arkansas

QUILT BLOCKS go wild!

10+ fun & funky projects
by Eleanor Levie & Celebrity Quilters

Library of Congress Control Number: 2011934167
ISBN-13: 978-1-60900-417-0

We have made every effort to ensure that these instructions are accurate and complete. We cannot, however, be responsible for human error, typographical mistakes, or variations in individual work.

LEISURE ARTS, INC.

EDITORIAL STAFF
Editor-in-Chief: Susan White Sullivan
Quilt Publications Director: Cheryl Johnson
Special Projects Director: Susan Frantz Wiles
Senior Prepress Director: Mark Hawkins
Art Publications Director: Rhonda Shelby
Imaging Technician: Stephanie Johnson
Prepress Technician: Janie Marie Wright
Publishing Systems Administrator: Becky Riddle
Mac Information Technology Specialist: Robert Young

BUSINESS STAFF
President and Chief Executive Officer: Rick Barton
Vice President of Sales: Mike Behar
Director of Finance and Administration:
    Laticia Mull Dittrich
National Sales Director: Martha Adams
Creative Services: Chaska Lucas
Information Technology Director: Hermine Linz
Controller: Francis Caple
Vice President, Operations: Jim Dittrich
Retail Customer Service Manager: Stan Raynor
Print Production Manager: Fred F. Pruss

BOOK PRODUCER:
Eleanor Levie, Craft Services LLC, EleanorLevie.com

BOOK DESIGNER:
Diane Pizzuto, PZZT! Graphic Design, pzztdesign.com

ASSOCIATE EDITOR:
Valerie L. Egar, v873@hotmail.com

COVER & FULL-PAGE PHOTOGRAPHY:
Donna H. Chiarelli Studio, dhcstudio.com

ILLUSTRATOR:
Rachel Shelburne, rachel@sdr0.com

introduction

The classic quilt block: Our cherished legacy. And now, the perfect inspiration for your creativity. The book you hold in your hands: A collection of fresh, modern quilt projects made with quilt blocks that are twisted and tweaked, sliced and skewed.

Five extraordinary quilters famous for innovation join me to show you, in 10 fabulous projects, how easy it is to transform trad into rad, the past into a blast.

These projects will rock your style. 10+...the plus sign stands for additional variations, but also signifies that you can take any of the blocks and use them in any of the projects. Consider these ways to multiply the possibilities:

- Supersize a split log cabin to make pillows for your cabin or castle (see pages 17 and 46).

- Go crazy with stars to make a table runner shine (see pages 50 and 17).

- Play the queen of hearts with a realm of wonky hearts on a quilt big enough to spread on a king-size bed (see pages 24 and 39).

You get the picture. And setting the blocks into different projects is just the beginning. You'll find lots of workbooks—well, playbooks(!) scattered about, chock-a-block with hands-on exercises. Here's where you discover how to jumpstart your creativity and rise to a whole new level of original quilt design. You'll also find tips and tricks for selecting your own colors and fabrics, guaranteeing spectacular results to accent that special spot in your home, or carry proudly on your arm.

Soooo, take Granny's quilt block and kiss tradition good-bye.

Get ready, get set, go wild!

Eleanor Levie

contents

NINE PATCH / *goes to pot*

by Eleanor Levie

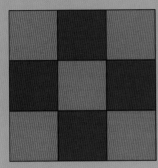

Classic Nine-Patch block

I swore I would never make a potholder. Why? Because one too many people called my extremely labor-intensive mini-quilt a "potholder." That burned! Add to that the fact that my potholders get stained and scorched in no time flat. Whatta way to treat my quilting! Well, I now know that potholders are a totally cool way to try out a new block... or in this case, a way to turn up the heat on an old block. No reason to fret—it's just a potholder. This "recipe" simultaneously cooks up two potholders in a flash.

Size: 8" square

what you'll need

- Cotton fabrics:

  2 contrasting 9½" squares, for the tops

  2 coordinating 9½" squares, for the backs

  1 fat eighth each of 2 striped fabrics, for binding

- Thermal batting, four 9½" squares

- Cotton batting, two 9½" squares

- Variegated machine quilting or topstitching thread

- Buttons to coordinate with fabrics: ⅞"–1" sew-thru buttons, plus smaller contrasting buttons

knock off the block

1 Neatly stack 2 contrasting 9½" squares. Cut the square into approximate thirds by making 2 angled cuts (see a).

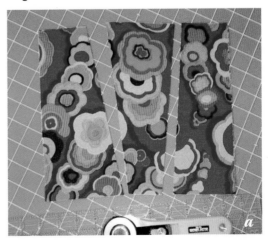

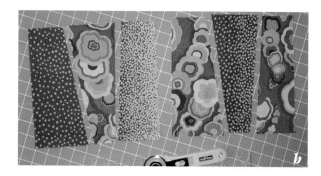

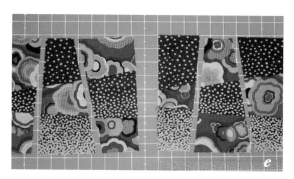

2 Set the 3 pieces of the top layer aside. Swap the center sections between the two blocks (see b). Stitch the 3 pieces of each new block together (c). Press the seam allowances toward the center.

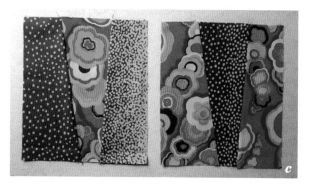

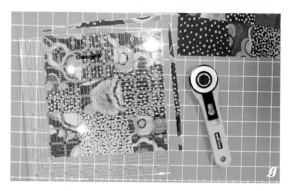

3 Restack the two new blocks with the seams going in the same direction. Cut the square into approximate thirds by making 2 angled cuts across the seams (d).

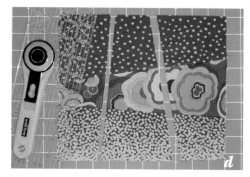

put one together

1 Place a 9½" square, for backing, right side down on work surface. Layer two 9½" squares of thermal batting, Mylar sides facing out, plus one layer of cotton batting in between, on top. (*Note:* The cotton batting will absorb condensation.) Center a skewed Nine-Patch block on top. Pin the layers to secure, then machine-quilt.

spiro-gyro

Stitch a big spiral using the heaviest thread that'll fit your machine needle. Or, and try a random free-motion pattern. After all, it's just a potholder—not an heirloom quilt!

4 Set the 3 pieces of the top layer aside. Take the center sections, and re-press the seam allowances in the opposite directions–toward the sides. Then swap these sections between the two blocks (e). Join sections: place sections together with right sides facing, and pin to match the seams. Stitch to form a skewed Nine-Patch (f). Press and trim, squaring to 8" (g).

2 Zigzag-stitch along the edges of the Nine-Patch block. Trim batting and backing even with the block.

3 Following the Binding Action instructions in Quiltmaking Basics and using striped fabric, cut binding strips and piece to a 46" length. Position a straight-cut binding end at a corner on the front of the block, and sew binding along the edges, mitering corners as you go. When you get back to the starting point, encase the raw end, and leave the remaining binding strip long. Pin the folded edges of the binding to the back. Fold the long, remaining binding strip lengthwise into fourths with raw edges inside, for a hanging loop. Topstitch to secure (see photo h), trim to 8", bring it around in a loop, and tuck the raw end under the binding edge on the back; pin.

4 No need to hand-stitch the binding on the back of the potholder! Instead, use this quick, fun, and durable finish: Using the same thread as for quilting and a wide zigzag stitch, sew along the binding on the front (see photo i). Not only does this secure the edges of the binding on the back, but this stitching also secures the loop.

5 Stack and stitch 2 buttons at the corner with the loop. •

playbook

Freehand cutting make you flustered? Then take time first to draw wonky Nine-Patches, skewing each inside line of the tic-tac-toe format. Redraw your fav on large sheet of freezer paper marked with a 9½" square. Be sure to leave at least ½" between pieces. Cut out and press just the middle strips on fabric to guide your vertical and horizontal cuts.

9½"

9½"

BASKET / *goes bonkers*

by Eleanor Levie

Don't you just love baskets? They're such a charming way to show off a pot of geraniums or the pine cones you just couldn't resist. Baskets have graced American quilts throughout our history, in wholecloth heirlooms, Baltimore Albums, crazy quilts, and scrap quilts. Here, the traditional block gets stretched, skewed, and tilted so it seems to tap-dance across a table…yet it still keeps its day job as a receptacle. Two trapezoids partner as pockets to hold mail, jewelry, doggie treats, or any treasures you want at-the-ready.

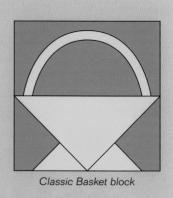

Classic Basket block

Size for wall hanging: 21" x 39"

what you'll need

- Cotton fabrics:

    1 fat quarter each of bright yellow and light yellow prints, for basket

    8" squares of 4 different green and orange prints, for Nine-Patch blocks

    Fat quarters and ½ yard cuts of various bright prints to audition as backgrounds, pockets

    ½ yard of heavy-weight decorator fabric or canvas, for backing

- Freezer paper

- Fusible batting, such as Fusiboo,* 25" x 44"

- Heavy fusible interfacing such as Peltex II,* 8" x 10"

- ¼ yard of fusible web, 18" wide

- Tear-away stabilizer, 8" x 20"

- Machine quilting or topstitching thread

- Orange rayon thread, 30 weight

- Rickrack in assorted colors and widths

- 3 jumbo buttons in assorted colors*

See Resources on page 64

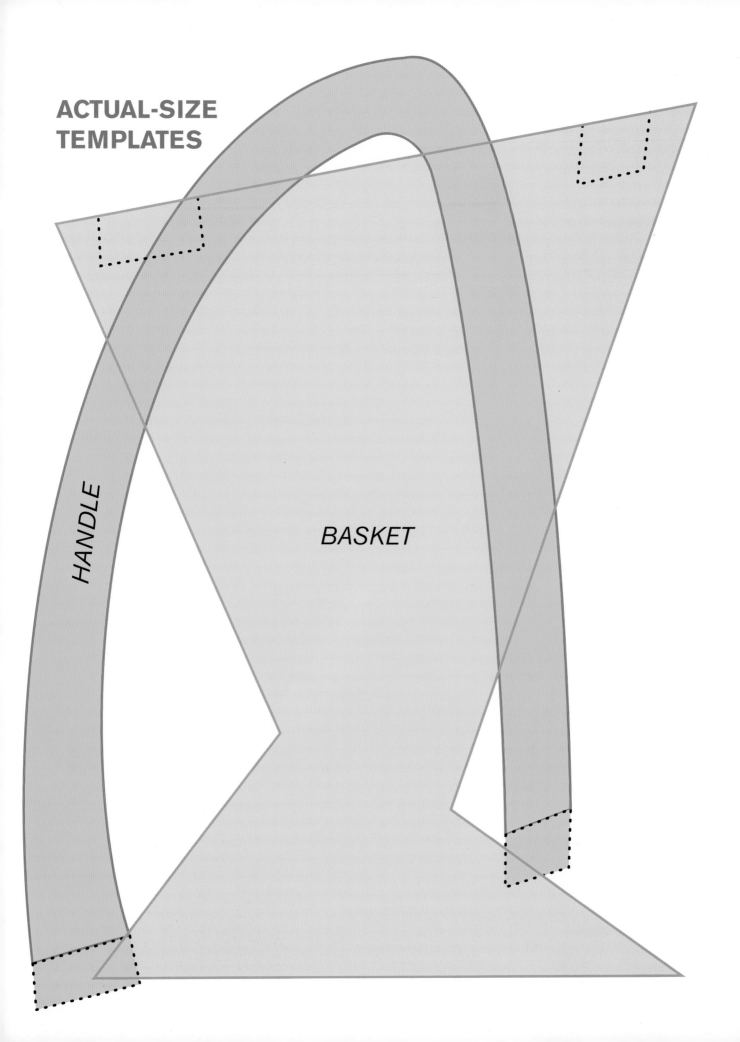

ACTUAL-SIZE
TEMPLATES

HANDLE

BASKET

basket

1 Trace actual-size templates for basket and handle onto matte side of freezer paper. Cut them out along the lines, including extended handle ends, as indicated by dotted lines, which will be overlapped by basket rim.

2 For basket front, place freezer paper basket template, shiny side down, on right side of bright yellow print. With a dry iron, press to secure. Cut out about ½" beyond pattern edges. Press onto rough side of heavy fusible interfacing, following manufacturer's instructions. Cut out along solid lines, using a rotary cutter and ruler for long, straight lines, and sharp scissors for inside angles. Remove freezer paper template and set aside to use later. Remove clear plastic from reverse of interfacing, and press wrong side of light yellow fabric onto it. Cut edges even with bright yellow front.

3 Using matching thread, machine-quilt basket, either following lines of print, making a diagonal grid, or creating another overall pattern. Then work a fine, medium-width zigzag, or satin-stitch, all around the basket. See photo a. Set this piece aside.

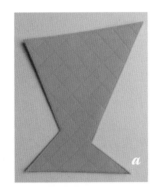

4 Press paper-backed fusible web to 8" x 10" pieces of light yellow fabric and bright yellow fabric. Press freezer paper basket template on front of light yellow fusible-backed fabric. Cut out along freezer paper template. Press freezer paper handle template to right side of bright yellow fabric; cut out along freezer paper outlines, including dotted-line extensions. Set these pieces aside.

background

1 Make 2 pairs of Nine-Patch blocks following the how-to's on pages 7 and 8, starting with 8" squares and finishing at 6½" squares, including seam allowances (see photo b). Alternate blocks and stitch together into a row.

2 Once you've created the Basket and Nine-Patch row, audition fabrics for backgrounds and pockets. Check out "A Material Whirl" on pages 14 and 15. Don't forget to consider where this pocketed piece will hang, and bring in some of the colors that appear in that space.

3 When you are happy with fabrics you have chosen and their placement, cut "wallpaper" fabric piece 16" x 18". Cut "tablecloth" 16" x 6½". Stitch together along one 16" edge and press seam allowances toward tablecloth.

4 Lay wallpaper and tablecloth on a flat surface. Measure 3" from the right edge along wallpaper/ tablecloth seam; mark with a pin. Place Nine-Patch row face down on top at a vertical tilt; see photo c. Insert a pin through the seam between the third and bottom block, ¼" from the right side edge, and then through the point marked with a pin on the background. Stitch along Nine-Patch row, ¼" from edge. Then trim away excess fabric, and press seam allowances toward Nine-Patch row.

5 Trim top and bottom edges so they are even and square. Cut fabric 19" x 14" for bottom panel. Stitch to tablecloth and Nine-Patch edge. Cut 22" x 9" fabric for top panel; stitch to wallpaper and Nine-Patch edge. Fold it in half lengthwise; as top half will become the sleeve (d). Trim fabrics to follow slant of right edge.

pick pocket position

1 Try out various positions for the basket front and handle, as in photo e. When you're satisfied with the composition, make it permanent as follows. First, fuse handle in place. Pin or baste tear-away stabilizer behind handle and where basket will be. Using orange thread, satin-stitch along handle edges (f).

2 Fuse light yellow basket to background, covering ends of handles. Satin-stitch around it with matching thread.

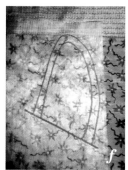

A MATERIAL *whirl*

How do you decide which fabrics find their way into your project? Which colors are too timid? Which printed fabrics patterns add punch? No need to put all your design options in one basket! That is to say, don't limit yourself. Once you have one or two fabrics you love for your project, it's easy to audition other colors and visual textures to see which ones work best.

For Basket Gone Bonkers, I was inspired by Ella Fitzgerald's version of the 19th century nursery rhyme:

> *A-tisket, a-tasket*
> *I lost my yellow basket.*
> *Won't someone help me find my basket*
> *and make me happy again?*

With Ella's song in mind, I chose a bright yellow fabric and made the basket for the main pocket. I knew the yellow basket would be the focal point for the wall hanging, so I chose bright prints that weren't predominantly yellow to make a row of Nine-Patch blocks.

First I thought I would use the Nine-Patch blocks as a checkerboard tablecloth underneath the basket. But when I took a step back to look, I found the scale and bold color overpowered the basket. I moved the blocks around on my design wall and found that placing the blocks next to the basket balanced the composition and created a cool vertical echo. I tilted the basket—wow! A sense of movement and whimsy. Now it was time to audition the fabrics I would use for the rest of the wall hanging. This is always my favorite part: I can be wild! I can be crazy! I went into my fabric stash and found a pile of fabrics to try. Again, no limitations. Sometimes, the most unlikely color turns out to be the one that makes the quilt sing.

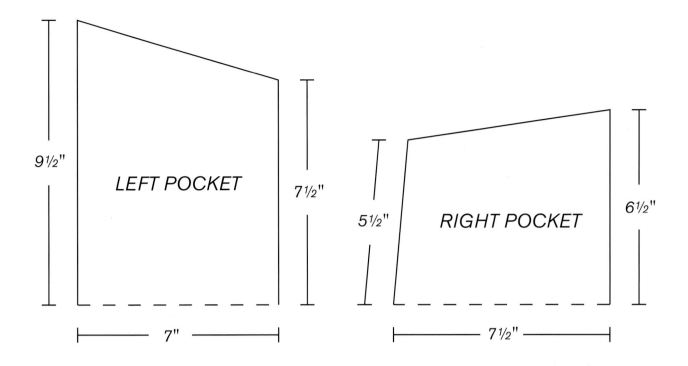

9½"

LEFT POCKET

7½"

7"

5½"

RIGHT POCKET

6½"

7½"

I like the high-energy brights in this version, and the way the blue print contrasts with the yellow basket. But maybe blue and yellow are too traditional? And basket doesn't integrate with the other colors. Also, bottom pockets seem boring in shape and placement.

Bottom pockets here are a lot more interesting. I like the purple mottled fabric as a less traditional background for the yellow basket, but too many colors makes the composition seem disjointed. And hoo boy, too many stripes.

I like how this chartreuse background fabric for the basket merges with the Nine-Patch blocks. But the fabric at the top? Wavy lines of that rickrack fabric are too close in style to the stripes directly below the basket. The big spot print for the bottom right pocket commands too much attention.

A sloppy version of what's materializing. I've balanced complementary, offbeat shapes, angled the right side, and tweaked the basket base. Fabrics work for me now, more or less. I'll play with trimmings...and nail down now which ones I will be using later. That way, I can hide the ends in the seams and avoid finicky finishing later.

Before you attach the basket front to the quilt, consider whether you'd like any embellishments or enhancements. This is your last opportunity to machine-sew orange rickrack or braided trim, or to add decorative machine stitches.

pockets on the docket

1   Pin basket front to basket back fused to background, letting top edge of basket front bow out a bit. Satin-stitch along side and bottom edges with a wider stitch.

2   For 2 patch pockets, fold chosen fabrics in half, right side in. Referring to each diagram on page 15, measure along the fold for bottom edge, and cut along sides and top edges. Stitch along sides, ¼" from edge, clip bottom corners, and turn each pocket right side out. Turn top edges ¼" to the inside, and press. Stitch rickrack over top edge, closing that edge. Pin pockets to background, skewing as desired. Topstitch along sides and bottom, ⅛" from edge and again ¼" from edge.

quilting

1   Referring to Quiltmaking Basics, sandwich the quilt top—excluding top 4"—with fusible batting and a firm decorator fabric or canvas for the backing.

2   For added punch, work all machine quilting with a heavy, variegated thread. First, echo-quilt around the basket and handle. If desired, quilt dense vertical lines along basket back.

3   Free-motion quilt a spiral on each Nine-Patch block, then add curves in between spirals.

4   Quilt tablecloth and bottom panel following the stripes, paisley design, or whatever fabric pattern is featured in your chosen fabrics.

finishing

1   Trim all edges even, and square up all but slanting right side edge.

2   Add flat trims such as rickrack at top and bottom.

3   For a facing, cut two 2½"-wide strips across entire width of fabric and one 2½"-wide strip 17" long. Referring to Quiltmaking Basics, face the bottom edge, then the side edges.

4   Bring fabric of top panel over the batting and backing, and press. Fold side edges in and topstitch to hem. Fold long raw edge under ¼" and pin even with seam of top panel on front of quilt. Baste along edge, then topstitch along seam in front. In this way, you secure the edge of top panel on backing, and at the same time create a sleeve.

5   Sew jumbo buttons along trim on top panel. •

LOG CABIN / *split level*

by Pam Dinndorf

The all-American Log Cabin block brings to mind the pioneers of old, building a house log by log. Times have changed, but this is still the #1 quilt block to build—and modify. Pam Dinndorf tossed around the idea of splitting logs diagonally in half, then picked up paper, scissors, and pencil: "I shaded where darker values might go, looking for a wildly dynamic sense of movement." She found it when a series of boomerangs emerged, made even more exciting in purple and yellow fabrics. Build it and they will come—the compliments, that is!

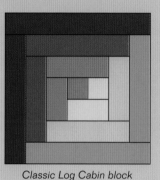

Classic Log Cabin block

Size: 12¼" x 64¾"

what you'll need

- Cotton fabric prints, batiks, hand-dyes, and woven stripes:

    ⅛ yard of red-orange, for hearthstones

    1 yard total of 10-12 yellows (or your choice of light color) in a variety of tints, shades, values, and types of pattern (geometric, floral, dotted, calligraphy, etc.), for logs

    1 yard total of 10-12 assorted purples (or your choice of dark color), for logs

    1 additional yard of any log fabric, for backing and facings

- Batting, 13½" x 66"

- Variegated thread, 30-40 weight, for quilting

- Foundation paper or vellum that goes through a photocopier; see Resources, page 64.

cutting

1. From red-orange fabric cut five 2¼" squares, for the hearthstone block centers (A).

2. From the designated fabric for the backing and facing, cut 14"-widths and piece to produce a 14" x 66" rectangle, for backing, plus two 2½" x 66" strips and two 2½" strips x 14" for facing. Set aside.

3. Cut 2½" strips as you go across width of yellow and purple fabrics to make foundation-pieced logs of desired colors and prints.

build the block

1. Trace, photocopy, or draft the foundation templates on pages 20 and 21. *Note:* These are the reverse of the quilt top design, as they

will be sewn to the wrong sides of fabrics. Use a copy machine to make 10 copies of templates on vellum or foundation paper. Rotary-cut foundation strips along the outlines. To save time, cut in multiple: stack 3 or 4 sheets neatly together, tape along the edges of the paper and staple as needed to keep sheets from shifting as you cut through the layers.

2   To complete logs for X and Y (which will also be used for Z), tape pieces together along the short dash lines.

3   Make each split Log Cabin block at a time, referring to the block diagram on page 20 for yellows and purples (or your choice of lights and darks), but choosing specific fabrics as you go. For center A, use one of the squares that have already been cut. Although you may choose to use the foundation, it's really not necessary. For all other split logs, create bisected rectangles of yellow and purple using foundation pieces as follows.

4   Begin with split log B and C: From 2½"-wide strips, one from yellow fabric and one from purple fabric, cut pieces at least ½" longer than diagonal line on B/C foundation—or at least 3¼" long. Place these fabric rectangles together with right sides facing, edges even, and yellow fabric on top. Position B/C foundation on top, covering all of patch B plus ¼" beyond: ¼" beyond diagonal dividing line, and at least ¼" extending beyond all corners. Pin layers to secure. Using a neutral-colored thread (red used here for readability) and a stitch length that is smaller than usual (10-12 stitches per inch), sew on the marked diagonal line between B and C. Extend the beginning and end of stitching line into seam allowances. See photo a.

5   Remove pin, flip piece over, unfold purple fabric piece, and press seam. Then flip piece back to show foundation and trim unit ¼" beyond the foundation paper to form the B-C split log, 2¼" x 2¼", which includes ¼" seam allowances all around. See photo b.

continued on page 22

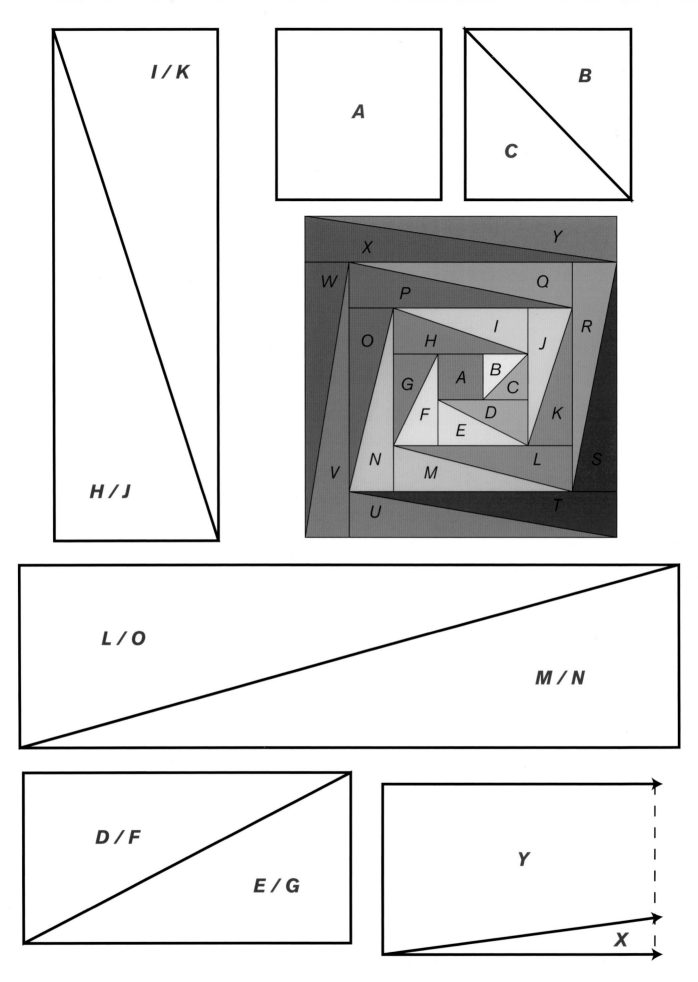

I / K

A

B

C

H / J

L / O

M / N

D / F

E / G

Y

X

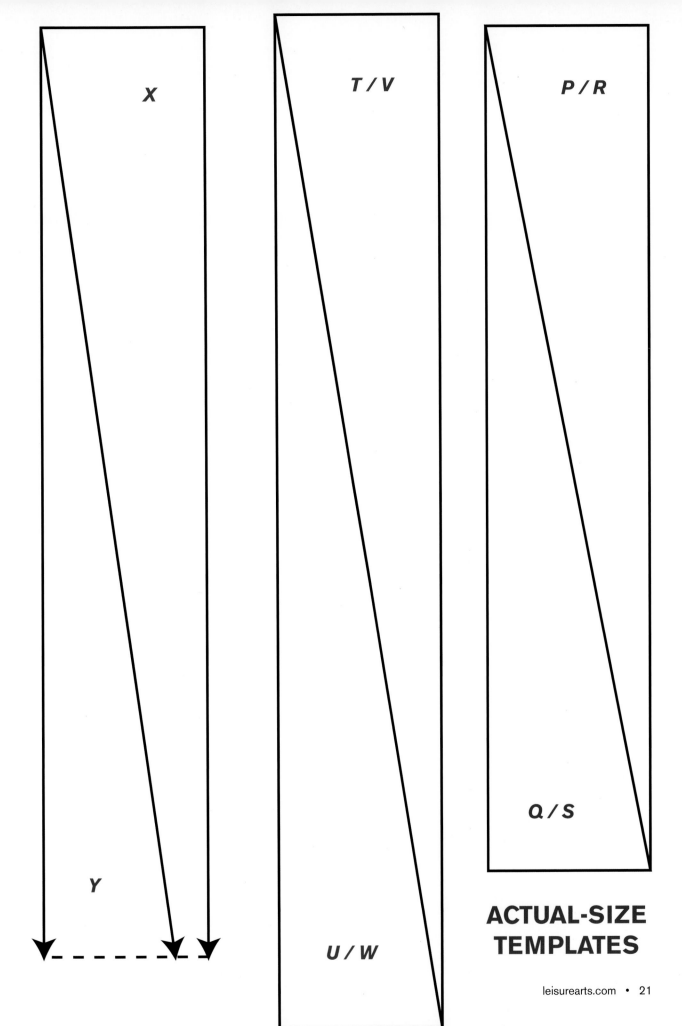

**ACTUAL-SIZE
TEMPLATES**

Want a '60s vibe? Grab a passel of black & white prints. Arrange 4, 9, 16, 25, or 36 Split Log Cabin blocks in a square. Optical illusion to the max!

6 For next split log D and E, use foundation piece labeled D/F and E/G—you will use another copy of the same foundation piece to construct the F and G split log. Also use the same purple fabric you previously used for patch C—this is for patch D, plus a new yellow fabric for patch E. Cut 2½"-wide strips to a length at least ¼" beyond the diagonal line on both sides for a purple and yellow rectangle 2½" x 4½". Place rectangles together with right sides facing and new yellow fabric E on top. Place foundation paper piece on top, with E completely on the yellow fabric, the marked diagonal line ¼" from long raw edges and centered between short sides. There should be at minimum ¼" beyond the corners of patch E. Pin to secure, and stitch along the diagonal, starting and ending ¼" beyond the foundation. See photo c. Press and trim as before; see photo d. The D-E split log will have dimensions of 2¼" x 4", which includes ¼" seam allowances all around. Now the center and 2 split logs are complete (photo e).

7 Continue in this manner, referring to Block Diagram on page 20 for colors, and working clockwise in alphabetical order. Most different-size foundation pieces serve to make 2 split logs. As you go, always use one fabric from the previous split log, plus a new fabric for the contrasting color. The placement of the same or different purple and yellow fabrics from one split log to the next will create the look of "boomerangs" in the corners throughout the block. Always place the yellow fabric on top, with the patch that will be yellow completely surrounded, and the patch that will be purple hanging off the edge. Always press from the back so that seam allowances are toward the purple patch. It gets easier as you go!

8 Arrange the split logs around the center square, referring to the Block Diagram, checking for consistent fabrics that form "boomerangs," and working in alphabetical order. Flip B-C log over onto A, with right sides facing, and stitch along the edges of foundation paper piece as shown in photo f. Fold out B-C, and press seam allowances toward A. Place back into the arranged layout, to keep all pieces in proper position. Flip D-E piece over onto the joined A-B-C piece. Insert pins at corners of foundation to ensure pieces are aligned. Stitch along the edges of foundation paper piece as shown in photo g. Fold out D-E and press seam allowances toward D (photos f and g).

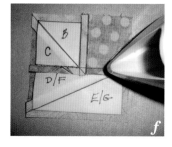 

After doing an entire round—or at regular intervals, sparingly trim edges of the growing block. Continue in this manner, always pressing toward the purple patch. When block is completely joined, pressed, and trimmed, it should measure 12¾" square—this includes ¼" seam allowances all around. Make 4 more blocks in this manner.

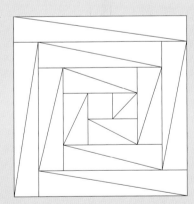

assemble the runner

1 Arrange the 5 finished blocks in a row. By varying position of blocks, you can create zigzags of yellow and purple down the runner—see photo on page 4. Stitch blocks together. Press seam allowances toward the darker fabrics.

2 To give runner the added kick of an unusual angle at each end, join a 2¼" x 12¾" strip that contrasts with the last fabrics to the ends. Cut each of these added strips diagonally in half.

3 Carefully remove all foundation paper. Following Quiltmaking Basics, sandwich the quilt top on batting and backing. Quilt along the yellow fabric close to but not quite in the ditch, using variegated thread. With most seam allowances pressed under the purple fabrics, padding them slightly, and the quilting stitches flattening the yellow areas, you'll have a noticeable contrast in dimensionality.

4 Finish the runner with a facing (see page 61). Begin with a strip at each end, and stitch along the ends and around the corners of the facing. Then pin on the long edges so they extend ½" beyond the previous lines of stitching. Clip the corners, and bring the facing to the back. •

playbook

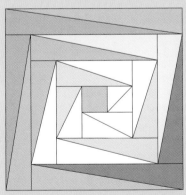
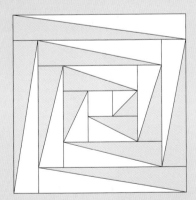
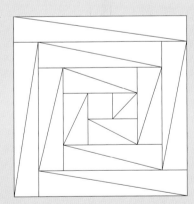

Make multiple enlarged photocopies of any of the blocks above. Color with colored pencils or markers to audition various color possibilities. Try various positions for light, medium, and dark values. Cut up a block and move pieces around, reversing some logs.

Make multiple photocopies of your favorite colored block. Instead of positioning blocks in a row, arrange them into a square of 3 by 3, or a rectangle of 4 by 6. Be open to interesting juxtapositions and surprising secondary patterns.

HEARTS /*askew*

by Elizabeth Rosenberg

"I'm known to wear my heart on my sleeve," admits Elizabeth Rosenberg, yet she avoids using hearts in her quilts, so as to project a stronger, less sentimental image. All the same, when assigned to create a heart design, she broke her resolve and went at the task whole-heartedly, injecting a quirky sense of fun that's *so* not sweet or frilly. Explosive jewel tones in hand-dyed fabrics and batiks give this wall hanging an off-the-wall punch.

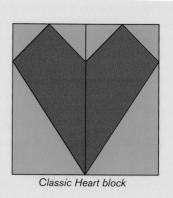

Classic Heart block

Size for wall hanging: 22" square

what you'll need

- Cotton fabrics:

  For each of 5 different colors, 3 different bright tone-on-tone prints or batiks; for example, 3 yellow-gold fabrics: one mottled, one dotted, and one striped; 2/3 yard of one fabric, a fat quarter for the other
  2 fabrics in that color

  Fabric for backing: 24" x 30"

- Batting, 24" square

- Variegated thread, 30-40 weight, for quilting

- Freezer paper

block pattern

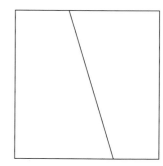

1   On the matte side of a sheet of freezer paper, draw a 6" square.

2   For the quilt classic, a vertical line—the center axis—divides block exactly in half, and heart halves are mirror images. See illustration at top right. For a skewed heart, start by drawing an angled axis that divides square roughly in half.

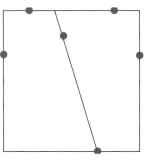

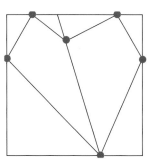

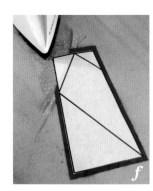

3 Randomly mark a dot along the top line to either side of the axis, and a dot along each side line. Then mark a dot along the axis, closer to the top than the bottom; see above left.

4 Using a ruler, connect the dots to make a wonky heart, as shown above right.

hearts are wild

For each freezer paper foundation, vary the angle and location of the axis, and the position of the dots you'll connect. See playbook, page 31.

foundation piecing

1 Trim freezer paper along the marked square (see a). Cut block along the axis, dividing it in half.

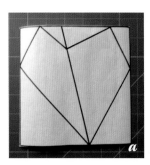

2 Place one half on a fabric selected for the heart, with the waxy side of the freezer paper on the wrong side of the fabric (with batiks and hand-dyes, use either side) and with at least ¼" of fabric extending all around. Press freezer paper to adhere it to fabric (see b), and trim fabric edges ¼" beyond the freezer paper edges (c).

3 Foundation-piece the 3 background sections around the half-heart as follows—it doesn't matter which area you do first. Cut a chunk of background fabric that's about ¾" larger than the background shape all around. Place it over the area you intend to cover, and make sure it extends completely over background shape and beyond, to provide seam allowances. Then, flip it over so it extends ¼" beyond line between heart and background, and pin it in place to keep it from slipping or shifting.

4 Turn to marked, matte side of freezer paper. Using a closer than usual stitch (10-12 stitches per inch), sew along marked line between the heart and background section. Extend the beginning and end of stitching line into seam allowances (see d).

5 Peel back and fold freezer paper toward axis. Trim heart and background fabric ¼" beyond marked line (see e). Then, unfold the background piece, and press freezer paper back in place (see f).

6 Repeat this process to cover each background shape on half the heart block. Trim half block to ¼" beyond outer freezer paper edges (see g).

7 Repeat steps 2 through 6 to foundation-piece other half of the block (see h).

8 Place the two half blocks together, with right sides facing and with the two axis edges aligned. Sew along the axis, extending line of stitching into seam

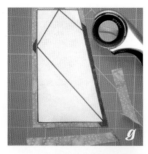

4 Add a different-color border on each side, auditioning colors to find the best contrast. Cut strips 2½" wide; join to top and bottom, then to sides. Press and square up the quilt top.

assemble wall hanging

1 Peel off all freezer paper.

2 Refer to the Quiltmaking Basics and sandwich the quilt top on batting and backing. Quilt—here, an all-over pattern of hearts and loops in variegated thread makes an easy free-motion pattern.

3 Trim and add binding, using the color fabric not used for borders, and insert a sleeve along the top edge. •

allowances at top and bottom (see i). Press seam allowances of axis to one side. Trim block ¼" beyond marked edges of freezer paper square. Leave freezer paper in place until you assemble the blocks, since it will stabilize them and keep them square. Photo j shows a finished block.

assemble the quilt top

1 Make seven 6" heart blocks (6½" including ¼" seam allowances all around), using same color but a different fabric for each half heart, and for backgrounds of each side.

2 Follow previous directions but start with a marked 3" square. Make eight 3" heart blocks, which will be combined to form two Four-Patch heart blocks.

3 Arrange the 6" blocks and foursomes of 3" blocks into 3 rows of 3. Move blocks around until you are happy with the balance of colors. Then stitch the 3" blocks into rows, and press seam allowances toward the darker background fabric. Sew the rows together, and press seam allowances downward. In the same way, stitch the 6" blocks and Four-Patch blocks together in rows, and then stitch the rows together.

HEART / *of bold*

by Elizabeth Rosenberg

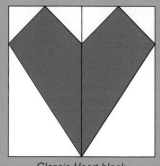

Classic Heart block

Take a walk on the wild side! Surround one wonky, wonderful heart with animal-skin prints, and bag yourself a public statement of your personal style. Art quilter Elizabeth Rosenberg grazed through her collection of zebra-striped fabric, which she jokes about "using in my spare time to cover every surface in my home." Here, one print is the perfect antidote for a heart that's skewed, but which may still reflect certain goody-two-shoes tendencies. Another zebra pattern stripes up the lining. Add a hodgepodge of white buttons and you're off to hunt down adventure!

Size: 13½" x 14" x 3½" deep

what you'll need

- Cotton fabrics:

  1 fat quarter each of 2 different fuchsia fabrics (shown here, one batik and one mottled hand-dyed), for heart and bag exterior

  1 fat quarter of small-scaled zebra stripe or other animal print, for block background

  ¼ yard of black, for sashing frame and handles

  ½ yard of muslin for backing

- ½ yard of zebra striped or other animal print, for lining and optional interior pockets

- Batting such as Nature-Fil Blend Quilt Batting from Fairfield Processing (see Resources on page 64), 36" x 48" piece

- Variegated thread, 30-40 weight, for quilting

- Assorted white sew-thru buttons, ³/₈"–⁷/₈" in diameter

- Freezer paper

cutting

1 To use fabrics most economically, cut large pieces first. Cut 14" x 17" rectangles, 1 from batik, for bag back, 2 from zebra print, for lining, and 2 from zebra or other fabric, 14" x 12½", for interior pocket.

2 From black fabric, cut handles: 2 strips 4½" x 18". Set aside.

3 From batting, cut two 16" x 18" rectangles and two 4" x 18" strips.

have a heart

1 Follow directions for the 6" block in Hearts Askew on pages 24-27. Use one fuchsia fabric for one side of heart, the second fuchsia fabric for other side, and a small-scale zebra-stripe fabric as your background. Remember to cut fabrics at least ½" larger than area you are covering and to allow fabric to extend at least ¼" beyond marked outlines of freezer paper all around.

2 When you have pieced 2 half-blocks, place them together, with right sides facing and with the 2 axis edges aligned. Sew along the axis, extending line of stitching into seam allowances at top and bottom. Press seam allowances of axis open, to avoid bulk. Trim block ¼" beyond marked edges of freezer paper square to make a 6½" block. Leave freezer paper in place for now.

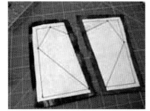

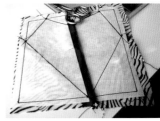

3 For the following how-to's, pin pieces together with right sides facing, stitch with fuchsia sewing thread, and press seam allowances outwards from the center. First, add sashing strips all around block: From black fabric, cut 2½"-wide strips, two 6½" long and two 10½" long. Join the shorter strips to top and bottom of heart block; join a longer strip to each side of block.

4 Complete the bag front: From hand-dyed fabric, cut a strip 4¼" x 10½". Sew to bottom of block, pressing as before. From each fuchsia fabric, cut a 3" x 14¼" strip, and join to sides of block and bottom section. From batik, cut a 3"-wide strip to fit across top of bag front; stitch and press.

assemble the bag

1 Trim rectangle for bag back to same size as bag front. Cut 2 pieces each of batting and muslin 1" larger all around than bag front and back. Following Quiltmaking Basics, sandwich the layers, centering the bag front on muslin and batting. Repeat, centering bag back on second layer of batting and muslin. Quilt both pieces. Here, Elizabeth used variegated thread to stitch a ½" grid over both pieces.

2 Place bag front and bag back together with right sides facing and stitch along sides and bottom. Clip bottom corners and press seam allowances open. To "box" the bottom so the bag can stand

playbook

Sketch lots of skewed hearts, varying the slant of the axis and the shape of each side. Choose your fav for the heart of this project, and use them all for the Hearts Askew wall hanging... or for a quilt sized to your heart's content.

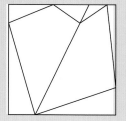 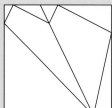 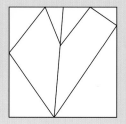

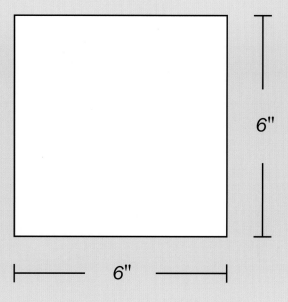

ready, aim, fire!

Why not shoot an arrow through your heart, using appliqué, thread painting, or couching? Cupid wouldn't want it any other way!

up, refer to the how-to's and photos on page 55, but measure, mark, and sew only 1¼" from the triangle peak that's formed.

3 Prepare an interior patch pocket as follows: Place two 14" x 12½" rectangles together, right sides facing, and stitch along one 14" edge. Turn to right side and press. Turn edge down 2", like a cuff, and topstitch. Pin to one lining rectangle, with top of the cuff edge 16" from bottom edge. Stitch across, 4" from bottom. Pin second lining rectangle on top, with right sides facing. Stitch along side and bottom edges. Box the bottom as described in previous step.

4 Fold top edges of bag and lining ¼" to wrong side and press. Set aside.

5 For handles, turn one long edge of each black fabric strip under ¼" and press. Place a 4" x 18" strip of batting centered on top. Fold long fabric edges to meet at the center with folded edge overlapping; press. Use variegated thread to quilt a line of stitching very close to the fold, and then 2 more parallel lines to either side. Pin ends of one handle to bag front, 2½" from side seams, and 1" below pressed rim. In the same manner, pin second handle to bag back. Insert lining in bag, wrong sides together and side seams aligned. Topstitch along top edge to finish top and secure handles in place. Reinforce ends of handles with added machine stitches along topstitching.

6 Sew buttons in assorted sizes onto the black sashing strips, using various colors of thread. Allow stitches to penetrate all layers, including the lining and pocket, to secure all layers. ●

RAIL FENCE *derailed*

by Tonya Ricucci

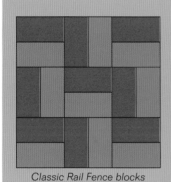

Classic Rail Fence blocks

Such an orderly block is the classic Rail Fence, and so fenced in! Tonya Ricucci broke free of constraints, taking her version off the rails. She sliced rectangles off-kilter, then combined slices to create a new frontier. Are those Sawtooth Mountains beyond the property line? Or a Streak o' Lightning in the skies above? Whether in bold solids with sharp flanges or in soft shirting fabrics with a wavy edge, these pillows will prove that there are no boundaries to your creativity!

Size: 18" square pillow, plus 2" straight flanges

what you'll need

- Cotton fabrics:
  - ¹/₃ yard each of reversible solids: red, turquoise, yellow
  - ½ yard of black with white dot, for pillow back and flanges
  - 12" x 24" rectangle of white with black spots, for pillow back
  - 22" square of muslin
- 22" square of fusible batting; Fusiboo* used here
- ¾ yard each of 2 different grosgrain ribbons, ⁷/₈"–1" wide
- 18"-square pillow form*
- 3 large decorative buttons

*See Resources on page 64

block pattern (pillow #1)

1 Cut 3⁵/₈" x 4½" rectangles from fabric: 19 red, 10 turquoise, and 9 yellow.

2 Place a red rectangle horizontally oriented on a turquoise one, with edges even. Position a ruler diagonally across width of rectangle, at least ½" from each side; cut. See photo a.

3 Referring to photos b and c on the next page, match top red piece on the left with bottom turquoise piece on the right (photo c). Stitch together, ¼" from edges.

don't fence me in!

Defy the convention of identical repeat blocks! Make each of your cuts on your rectangles a little different in angle and placement. Just don't cut straight up and down, and leave at least ½" on each side.

4 Press seam allowances toward red fabric. Lay on your work surface as shown in photo c. Note that seams are along top and bottom of block; Tonya calls this an up-down block.

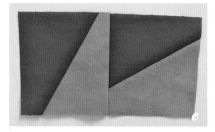

5 Turn remaining red and turquoise pieces to their reverse sides and sew together. Press toward the red. Lay out as shown in photo d, on the right side. Note that seams are along the sides; Tonya calls this a side-to-side block. Trim both the up-down block and the side-to-side block to 3½" square. Stitch the up-down block to the side-to-side block. When done correctly,

turquoise will seem to flow from one block to the next; see photo e. Make 7 more pairs, for a total of 8 red/turquoise block pairs.

6 In same manner, make 7 pairs of red and yellow blocks. Also make 2 more pairs of red/ turquoise blocks and 2 more pairs of red/yellow blocks, but don't stitch these last 4 pairs of blocks together—they will be used as single blocks.

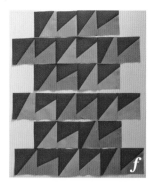

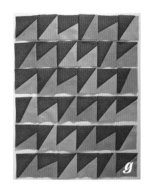

7 Arrange block pairs as shown in photo f. Fill in with single blocks as shown in photo g. Sew blocks together into rows. Press seam allowances toward the block without a seam on the side. Pin rows together, matching seams, then sew, removing pins as you go. Press seam allowances downward. See photo h.

assembly

1 Referring to Quiltmaking Basics, make a quilt sandwich with pieced top centered on batting and a muslin backing. Machine quilt in the ditch. Trim batting and muslin even with quilt top.

2 From black dot fabric, cut a 16" x 24" rectangle, for pillow back. Then cut 2½"-wide strips for

playbook

Copy one of these Rail Fence Derailed patterns several times, and use colored pencils to audition possible color combinations. Alternatively, enlarge this pattern to 18", taping photocopies together as needed. Mock up several blocks, adhering half-square triangles cut from fabric onto 3½" squares of paper. Make lots of color copies of these blocks, cut them out, and arrange them on the enlarged pattern, like a jigsaw puzzle where all the pieces are square. Capture the best candidates with a digital camera, and print them out to compare and guide the cutting and piecing for the pattern you choose.

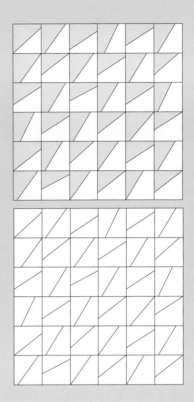

flanges: 2 strips equal in length to one side of quilted pillow top, and 2 strips 5" longer. Stitch first strips to top and bottom edges, and press seam allowances outwards. Stitch longer strips to sides, and press as before, then trim ends of strips even with top and bottom.

3 Make pillow back: turn ½" on one 24" edge of black dot rectangle to right side. Topstitch one grosgrain ribbon on top, covering turned raw edge of fabric. Place second grosgrain ribbon alongside the first, overlapping it slightly. Pin to secure and to mark locations for 3 buttonholes, long enough to accommodate buttons:

one at center, and 2 more, 3½" to either side. Zigzag-stitch to join ribbons, leaving areas designated for buttonholes unstitched (i).

4 With white spotted fabric, turn one 24" side ¼", then 1" to wrong side, for button placket. Topstitch and press. Overlap this placketed edge with grosgrain-covered edge, so that the combined piece measures 24" square. Pin flanged pillow front centered on top, with right sides facing and all edges even.

5 Stitch all around, ¼" from edges of pillow front. Trim pillow back even with pillow front. Clip corners. Unpin back pieces and turn pillow cover to right side. Press. Working from the front, stitch in the ditch along flange.

6 Stitch buttons on placket to correspond with buttonholes. Insert pillow form. ●

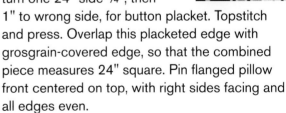

shirting variation

The pattern is wild, but the fabrics are mild in this pillow cover Tonya Ricucci made from shirting solids, stripes, and plaids. Raid your hubby's closet for that button-down that's seen better days. Scout thrift shops and tag sales for men's shirts. Sift through your stash for homespun. Shirting fabrics are reversible—any color or pattern is woven in, making them perfectly suited for use in this design, just as the bold solids previously showcased fit the bill. That recycled shirt provides a softness that's just right for hand-quilting. A ready-made button placket makes this pillow cover easy to put on over a pillow form, and take off when you wish to launder the cover. You just might get a freebie pocket, too!

Size: 18" square plus 4" scalloped flanges all around

what you'll need

- Cotton fabrics:

  Shirt that's ready to be recycled

  Other old shirts or small amounts of shirting fabrics: solid, striped, and plaid

  ¼ yard each of 4 black & white prints, for scalloped flanges

  ½ yard of black with white dot, for flanges on pillow back

  22" square of muslin

- 22" square of cotton batting
- Natural hand-quilting thread
- Assortment of shirt buttons

flirting with shirting (pillow #2)

1 Cut a 19" square from shirt front, including button placket and pocket. See photo j. Use the remaining fabric from the shirt for Rail Fence patches.

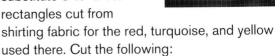

2 Follow the how-to's for block pattern on pages 33–34. However, substitute 3⅝" x 4½" rectangles cut from shirting fabric for the red, turquoise, and yellow used there. Cut the following:

19 – from a solid (substituting for the red)

10 – from a striped shirt (standing in for the turquoise)

9 – from a plaid shirt (taking over for the yellow)

3 Pair a solid rectangle with a striped one, keeping the solid color on top. Follow the directions for the red and turquoise blocks in steps 2, 3, and 4 on pages 33 and 34; make 8 pairs of blocks.

4 In the same manner, make 7 pairs of solid/plaid blocks.

5 Next, make 2 more pairs of solid color/striped blocks and solid color/plaid blocks, but don't stitch these together—they will be used as single blocks.

6 Arrange blocks referring to photo k, and stitch them together, referring to step 6 of block pattern and step 1 of assembly, page 34.

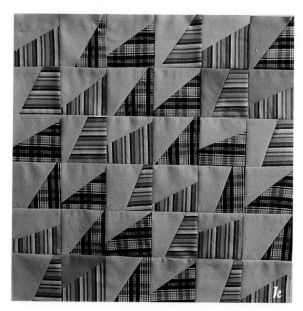

7 Hand-quilt along the solid patches, using quilter's masking tape to keep lines straight.

assembly

1 Trim pillow back featuring button placket even with quilted pillow front.

2 Cut 5"-wide strips from black & white prints, for flanges on front: 2 strips equal in length to one side of quilted pillow top, and 2 strips 10" longer. Stitch first strips to the top and bottom edges, and press seam allowances outwards. Stitch longer strips to sides, and press as before.

3 Cut four 5"-wide strips from black dot, for flanges on the back: 2 strips equal in length to one side of the button-placket pillow back, and 2 strips 10" longer. Stitch and press as before.

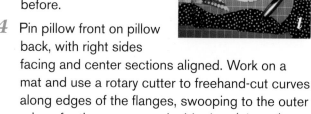

4 Pin pillow front on pillow back, with right sides facing and center sections aligned. Work on a mat and use a rotary cutter to freehand-cut curves along edges of the flanges, swooping to the outer edges for the corners and midpoints (photo l).

5 Stitch along curvy edge, and clip close to stitching around any tight curves. Turn pillow cover to right side; press.

6 Insert pins to realign edges of pillow front patchwork with pillow back shirt section. Working from the front, stitch in the ditch along seam between patchwork and flange.

7 Stitch shirt buttons randomly over patchwork. Insert pillow form. ●

ANOTHER WAY
to wonky

Tonya says, "I am a huge fan of Gwen Marston's *Liberated Quilting*. One of her techniques is to recut blocks to make them wonkier. I used that trick on Rail Fence blocks and discovered that I had created lightning bolts. Woohoo!"

You can do this with any block. Just position a square acrylic ruler on an angle. Here's another example of recutting done with Pinwheel blocks.

 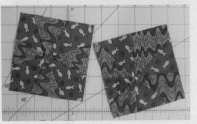

Try different angles and off-center placement to create a slew of skewed blocks, which come together to create a lively, whimsical composition.

There are downsides to this method: First, the new block will have a lot of bias edges. Working on foundation or a stabilizer such as interfacing will remedy that.

A second problem with re-cutting a block is that you end up with a smaller block, and there will be lots of fabric leftovers going into the waste basket.

Of course, Tonya saw the downsides and figured out a better way to make the skewed Rail Fence block. No bias, no recutting, and no scraps going to waste. Genius!

SQUARES / *out of square*

by Karla Alexander

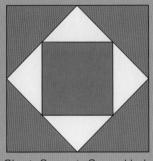

Classic Square-in-Square block

"Making blocks without any predetermined outcome—it's so much fun!" That's just one of the aces Karla Alexander deals out with her extraordinary "Stack the Deck" technique. Another is the chance to combine lots of different fabrics. And then there's shuffling the blocks around to create a totally unique and winning piece every time. So pick a palette, gather your fat quarters, and get ready for much more than a square deal!

Size: 42" x 62"; rectangular blocks, 6" x 8"; square blocks, 6" x 6"

what you'll need

- Cotton fabrics:

  Fat quarters of 1 purple print, 3 different pink prints, 3 different beige prints

  ½ yard each of 3 different black prints and 3 different gray prints

  3 yards of desired fabric for backing

  ½ yard of desired fabric for binding

- Batting, 48" x 68"

- Fabric pencil

cutting & stacking

1 Cut 56 rectangles 9" x 11" and 8 squares 9" x 9" from all the fat quarters and ½ yard cuts.

2 Choose 4 different rectangles that contrast greatly with each other (photo a, showing a different color palette) and stack them into a neat deck.

3 Refer to photo b, where a felt tip marker was used for readability, but use a fabric pencil and ruler to draw lines. First draw a line across the top right corner, connecting points loosely midway between

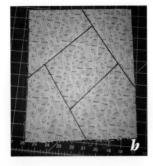

top and right side edges. Starting from this line, mark diagonally across top left corner. Starting from that line, mark across bottom left corner, and then connect points along first and third lines to mark across bottom right corner.

4 Cut on drawn lines in the same order you drew them. Then, using just the center section, mark lines across corners in same manner, and cut them out. See photos c and d.

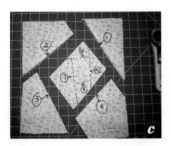

5 Take each corner piece from interior square (pieces 5, 6, 7 and 8) and put in same positions at bottom of deck. See photo e. Take top 2 layers of center "square" (it's really a quadrangle and not square at all) and place them on bottom of deck. See photo f.

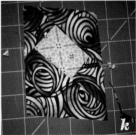

"square." Stitch ¼" from edge, unfold, and press seam allowances outward from center. Next add piece 7 to joined edge of center and piece 8 and press outward (photo g). Add piece 6, then 5, pressing as you go (photos h and i). Since your cuts were freehand, you'll often get dog ears and edges that don't line up perfectly. Press and then trim edges even, but don't worry about the corners being square and true (j and k).

2 Continue to work in reverse order to add pieces 4, 3, 2, and 1, pressing as you go (photo l). When block incorporates 3 different fabrics, it is complete. Now trim edges to make a 6½" x 8½" rectangular block with square, true corners.

stitching

1 This technique is similar to building a Log Cabin block; you will work in the reverse order from the cutting. Take piece 8, and flip it onto center

playbook

Take some time to mark possible cutting lines for rectangular and square blocks on same-size sheets of paper. Pin your favorites to decks and cut paper along the lines through the 4 fabric layers. Soon, you'll be ready to cut without marking, making each deck different, each block unique.

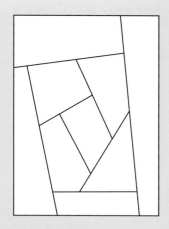 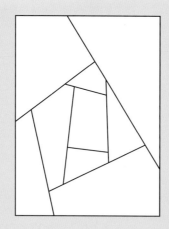 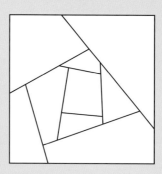 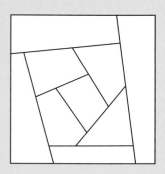

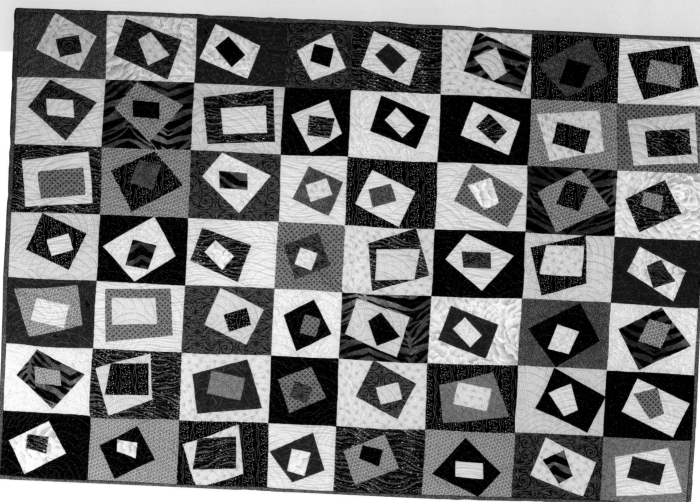

speed piecing

1   Once you've got the hang of this technique, you'll want to make 4 blocks at a time, using all pieces in deck. Working in reverse numerical order, join pieces in pairs without cutting thread. Chain-stitch all pieces numbered 8 to centers on that layer. See photo m.

2   Press piece 8 outwards, and cut thread between joined units (photo n). Retain same order as you chain-stitch piece 7 to previous units (o).

3   Restack the deck, in order to add piece 6 to each unit (p), then piece 5. Restack the deck and trim all combined center and middle rounds. Add piece 4 to each layer, restack, and trim the 4 edges simultaneously. Repeat for pieces 3, 2, and 1. Trim each block to 6½" x 8½", which includes ¼" seam allowances all around.

4   Continuing in this manner, layer 14 decks of 4 rectangles, to make 56 rectangular blocks. Vary the fabrics, striving for maximum contrast by using dark, medium, and light fabrics every time. Karla encourages, "Stay in charge! Don't settle! If at any point you want to add new colors or cuts—go for it!" Cut each deck slightly differently, so that each Square-in-Square composition is unique. See the playbook on the opposite page for inspiration.

5   Using the same method, start with 9" squares instead of 9" x 11" rectangles. Make 2 decks for a total of 8 squares, and trim them to 6½" square, which includes ¼" seam allowances all around.

assembly

1   Work on a design wall; see page 58. *Note:* You'll have 7 blocks more than needed, so you can decide which ones work best where, and use the leftovers in another project. Karla arranged the 7 square blocks in a row across the center, with 3 rows of 7 rectangular blocks above the squares, and 4 rows below. Use the row of squares anywhere you like! Rearrange blocks until you are happy with the balance of colors and patterns.

2   Stitch blocks in each row together. On odd numbered rows, press seam allowances toward the left. On even numbered rows, press seam allowances toward the right.

3   Pin and stitch rows together, nesting seam allowances to get neat intersections between blocks. Press seam allowances downward.

4   Piece a backing so it measures 2" larger all around than the quilt top. (Note: if you're sending it out to a longarm quilter, check to find out how much extra all around she requires.) Referring to Quiltmaking Basics, sandwich the quilt top over batting and backing. Quilt as desired; for this piece, a curvy pattern of fans or clamshells is a really nice complement to the sharp angles of the piecing design.

5   For binding, cut 2½"-wide strips across full width of fabric. Following the how-tos on pages 60-61, attach the binding. ●

m

n

o

DRUNKARDS / *off the path*

by Malka Dubrawsky

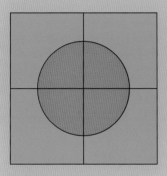

4 classic Drunkard's Paths

Downright intoxicating—that just might be what you think of Malka Dubrawsky's improvisational methods. For one pillow, create a quartet of imperfect circles, adding strips fairly randomly to make everything fit together. For the second pillow, supersize the beloved classic, surrounding warm colors with cool ones. Either way, you'll get high on a scrap-happy jumble of solids and prints. And if the prospect of curved piecing is a sobering thought, worry not. As Malka tells it, "Improvisation and curves go together like scotch and soda."

Size: 20" square

what you'll need

- Cotton fabrics:
  Small amounts of mostly solids and some prints; see individual designs for more specifics

  ½ yard of coordinating cotton solid or print, for backing

  ¼ yard of coordinating cotton solid or print, for binding

  Muslin, 24" square

- Cotton batting, 24" square

- 20" polyester zipper

- 20" square pillow form; used here: Feather-fil® Pillow Insert, 20" square from Fairfield Processing; see Resources on page 64

improvise it!

Note: For this design, you'll need assorted fabric scraps that are at least 6" square.

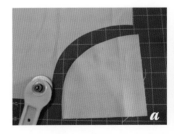
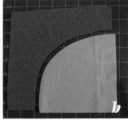

1 Lay a 6" square on a cutting mat, and working freehand, rotary-cut a quarter-circle as shown in photo a. Using cut arc as a template, cut a curved frame to fit the quarter-circle (photo b).

2 Fold each piece in half along curved edge to locate midpoint. Scissors-cut a little notch at the midpoint (photo c). Place both pieces together with right sides facing and with frame piece on top. Pin together, first at notched midpoints, then at each end, and then in between. Ease curved edges as you pin at close intervals (photo d). Stitch quarter-circle and frame together, leaving ¼" seam allowances and removing pins as you go. Press seam allowances toward frame (e).

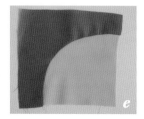

3 Repeat steps 1 and 2 to make a second quarter-circle unit (photo f). It may be necessary to beef up one of the blocks by adding a strip or strip-set to make both quarter circles the same size. Test-fit: Place blocks next to each other so quarter circles form a half circle. Note how in photo g, two small strips pieced together enlarge second quarter-circle so that both are same size. Pin both quarter-circle segments together with right sides

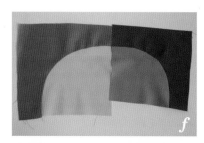

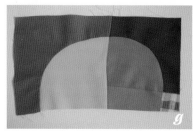

facing along adjacent edges. Stitch together, then press seam allowances toward the block with fewer seams (g).

4 Repeat steps 1-3 to make second half-circle segment. Add fabric strips as needed to ensure that half-circle segments are about equal in size and that arc edges meet. Pin half-circle segments together with right sides facing, along adjacent straight edge. Sew together, and press seam allowances toward side with fewer seams (h).

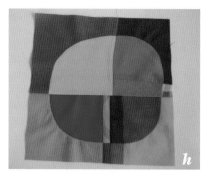

5 Repeat steps 1-4 three more times to make a total of 4 Drunkard's Path circles. Stitch together in pairs and press seam allowances to one side. Then stitch pairs together to form quilt top.

supersize it!

Note: For this design, you'll need a variety of mostly solid and print scraps and strips measuring 1¼" to 2½" in width. Select 6" to 9" lengths of warm colors—red, orange, rust, purple, and brown, and 4" to 6" lengths of cool colors—blue, turquoise, and green.

1 Photocopy or trace template A and half-template B on page 49. Fold a piece of paper in half. Place copy or tracing of B on paper with long dash lines along fold. Adding ¼" along all solid lines of each piece for seam allowances, cut out A and B. Unfold B to complete template. Label templates A and B.

2 Divide fabric strips into 2 piles, one for cool colors and a second for warm colors (see photo i).

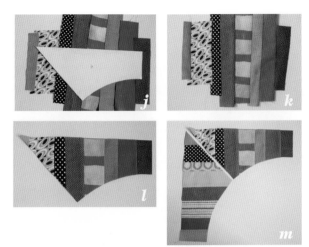

3   Begin with pile of cool-colored strips. Arrange strips vertically and slightly overlapping, so that when template A is placed on top, strips are perpendicular to longest straight edge and extend well beyond template on all sides (photo j). Stitch strips together as you have positioned them to make a unit large enough to fit template A. Press seam allowances in one direction (photo k). Pin template A on top and cut the strip-set even with template's edges (photo l).

4   Flip template A to reverse side. Following step 3, create another strip-set and cut out the reversed shape. Referring to photo m, position 2 A pieces together to form a corner and stitch them together along adjacent edges. Press seam allowances open.

5   Next, work with warm-colored strips and template B. Arrange strips vertically and slightly overlapping, with longest ones in the middle. Position template B on top like a Chinese fan (photo n), and make sure that strips extend well beyond the template on all sides. Stitch strips together as you have positioned them to make a unit large enough to fit template B. Press seam allowances in one direction. Pin template B on top and cut strip-set even with template's edges (photo o).

6   Fold the pieced, fan shaped B unit in half to locate the midpoint of the arc, and mark it with a pin. Pin the joined A units on the B unit, right sides

together, matching midpoints and corners, and easing edges. Pin generously (photo p). Stitch ¼" from edges, removing pins as you go. Press the seam allowances toward the A pieces (q).

7   Repeat steps 3 to 6 to make a total of 4 Drunkard's Path blocks. Rotate the blocks to form a circle. Stitch the blocks together in pairs, then stitch the pairs together, pressing seam allowances open to reduce bulk.

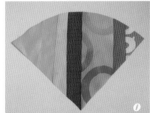

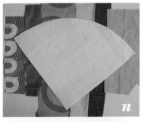

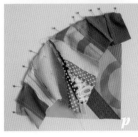

back on the path

1   Complete either pillow cover as follows. Referring to Quiltmaking Basics, sandwich pieced top on batting and muslin.

2   To quilt as Malka did, use white thread and begin at the center. Machine-sew a spiral, staying approximately a presser-foot's width away from the previous round. Continue in the corners, echoing the curves. Trim to 20½" square.

3   For a pillow back with a lapped zipper, cut pillow backing fabric 20½" x 30", then cut crosswise in half to make 2 rectangles, 15" x 20½". Refer to zipper manufacturer's instructions and apply two 20½" edges. Layer quilted pillow front on zippered back, wrong sides facing. Pin and trim pillow back to same size. For binding, cut 2½"-wide strips totaling 88". Following the how-to's on pages 60–61, piece and attach the binding.

4   Unzip the pillow cover and insert pillow form. •

button it up

For a zip-less finish, check out the how-tos for the pillow cover backs on pages 35 and 37.

playbook

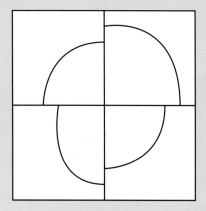 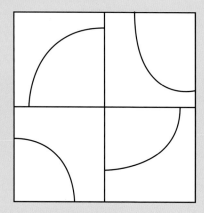 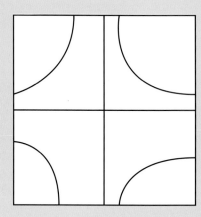

There's no reason why Drunkard's Path quarter-circles must be uniform, or come together to form a neat, smooth circle. Have fun on paper, or just improvise blocks and arrange them in different configurations.

ACTUAL-SIZE TEMPLATES

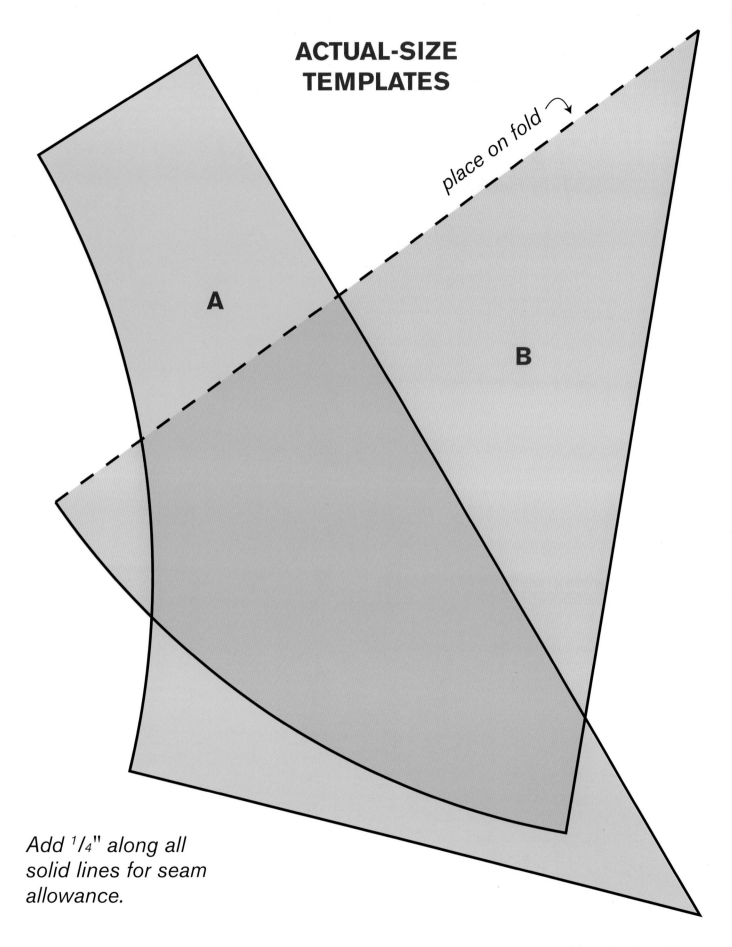

place on fold

A

B

Add ¹/₄" along all solid lines for seam allowance.

STAR / *partly crazy*

by Eleanor Levie

A traditional Star block calls for unerring geometry, precision piecing and perfect points. On the other hand, a wonky star winks, wiggles and dances. Polish up its sparkling personality with crazy-quilt piecing of metallic and satiny fabric and trims. Don't think this tote is just a pretty face–it's got secure pockets for your smart phone, glasses, keys, wallet, and other valuables, plus plenty of room for a little cardigan and a pair of comfy flats. Shine your star-power everywhere you go!

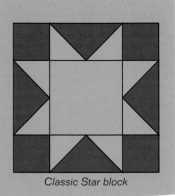
Classic Star block

Size: 21" across the rim, 17" high, not including the handles, and 5" deep

what you'll need

- Fabrics:

  ½ yard of 2 different heavy-weight fabrics, for upper and lower panels of bag exterior

  1 fat quarter cotton with metallic print, for star points

  1 fat quarter cotton gray solid, for star background

  Small amount of muslin

  Small amounts of assorted fancy fabrics, for crazy-piecing

  1 yard cotton metallic print, for lining (here, same as for star points)

  ¾ yard as desired, for interior pocket

- Short lengths of assorted trimmings

- 2¼ yards of gold piping

- Fusible batting such as Fusiboo,* 45" x 30" (half a crib quilt-size package)

- ½ yard of 2¼"-wide grosgrain ribbon in desired color (here, black)

- Bamboo purse handles, set of 2 half-moon shapes (these are vintage, but similar are available*)

- Magnet or frog (Chinese knot and loop) closures

- Assorted metallic and pearl buttons or charms

- Tracing paper and freezer paper

* See Resources on page 64

crazy star center (small front pocket)

1. Gather muslin and assorted fancy fabrics and trims; see photo a. Place an open toe, or appliqué foot on your sewing machine so you can easily switch between straight and zigzag stitching.

2. Trace actual-size crazy star center on page 53 (just the quadrangle; ignore arrows at this stage) onto tracing paper. Pin the marked tracing paper to fusible batting, and cut out along marked lines. Fuse to muslin (a thin, tan fabric shown here for readability), and cut out ¼" beyond the batting on all sides.

3. Using the lightest fabric and working freehand, scissors-cut a rough triangle that's about 1" on a side. Pin on the batting, off-center; see photo b.

4. Cut a chunk of another fabric with one edge at least 1¼" long. Place the piece right side down on the triangle so that this edge is even with the triangle's top edge, and extends beyond the triangle's corners. Stitch ¼" from the edge (see photo c). Flip this fabric over onto the right side and press. Place a trim over the seam and zigzag-stitch over it to couch it in place (photo d).

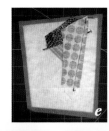

5. Cut a chunk of a third fabric with an edge that more than covers the right edge of the triangle plus the previous piece seamed to it. Place right side down on top, flush with the joined edges, with equal amounts extending at either end. Stitch, flip, press, and couch a strand of another trim over the new seam. See photos e and f.

6. Working clockwise, add new fabrics around the center patch, covering raw edges of the previous pieces, and embellishing each new seam with trim. Continue until the entire foundation is covered. Turn the piece over, and trim the edges even with the foundation. See photos g, h, and i.

7. Apply gold piping to the edges of the crazy-pieced quadrangle (j): Start and end at a corner, and lay piping flange along raw edges of quadrangle. Use a zipper foot and stitch close to piping. Next, place quadrangle right side down on print fabric, for inside of pocket. Stitch around edges, keeping zipper foot snugly against piping (k).

Leave 3" at center bottom edge open. Trim backing, clip corners, and turn to right side. Turn open edges to inside, and slip-stitch opening closed. Quilt crazy quadrangle. If desired, use

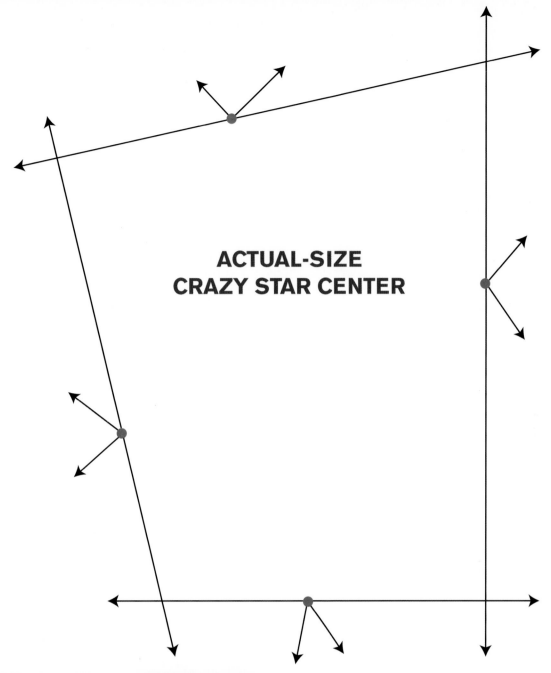

ACTUAL-SIZE
CRAZY STAR CENTER

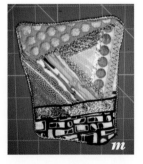

hitch your wagon to a star

Use the playbook on page 56 to draft your own unique star—traditional or wonky, square or quadrangle, big or little. Just make sure the pocket front fits in the center.

black thread to zigzag-stitch over piping, and to satin-stitch at corner where piping ends overlap, as well as one or two other spots. See photos l and m. You now have the completed crazy-pieced quadrangle, a pocket front that will be positioned over the center of a star block.

star block (large front pocket)

1 At about the center of a large sheet of freezer paper on the matte side, use a pencil and ruler to again trace actual-size crazy star center on page 53. Extend lines with arrows. Test-fit the crazy-pieced pocket front on the center, and redraw the freezer paper design if needed to accommodate it. Extend the top, bottom, and side lines 4". Extend the lines emanating from the red dots, completing the star points. Draw straight lines between the tips of the star points and extending to either side, forming a quadrangle. See photo n.

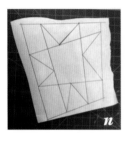

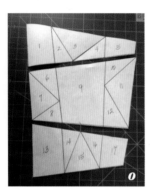

2 Trace a second crazy star pattern on freezer paper. Number the patches as shown in photo o and cut out the pieces on one pattern; use the other as a reference.

3 Use a hot, dry iron to press patch 9 (star center and back of front pocket) plus all even-numbered patches to a metallic cotton, for star points. See photo p. Press remaining patches to gray fabric, for the background (q). Cut patches ¼" beyond freezer paper edges (r).

evening star evening bag

Cut two quadrangles 1" larger all around than the star block. Stitch them together, pillowcase-style, and center the Star block on top. Stitch around sides and bottom, apply a closure, and add a shoulder strap. Now go dancing!

4 Pin adjacent pieces together with right sides facing; insert pins to align fabrics for precise points (s). Start by joining the 3 patches that make up middle of each side (t): 2-3-4, 6-7-8, 10-11-12, and 14-15-16. Press seam allowances outwards, toward star points. Add corners 1 and 5 to 2-3-4 unit, and add corners 13 and 17 to 14-15-16 unit, pressing as before.

Join center 9 in between 6-7-8 unit and 10-11-12 unit. You now have 3 rows; stitch rows together, pressing seam allowances toward center. See photos u and v.

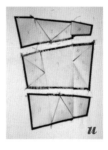

5 Place star block on batting and cut batting even with star block edges. Then trim batting ¼" smaller all around and center on wrong side of star block; fuse in place. Add piping and backing in same manner as for crazy star center. Quilt in the ditch around star points. Pin crazy star center

onto star block's center, and stitch in the ditch of the piping along sides and bottom edge to complete small pocket. If desired, zigzag-stitch over piping around star block as indicated for crazy star center.

assemble the bag

1 Create pattern, using a large sheet of paper and referring to diagram below. Start by drawing a 15" line centered at bottom of paper. From midpoint of this line, draw a vertical line 22" high. At top of vertical line, draw horizontal lines 11½" to the left and right. Connect ends of top and bottom lines. Draw a parallel line 10" from the bottom line.

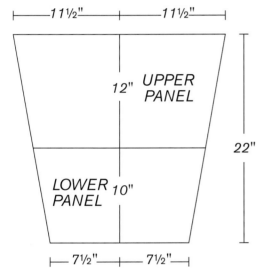

2 Using pattern you have just drafted, cut 2 pieces of batting, 2 fabric pieces for lining, and 2 more pieces of fabric for an interior pocket. Then use top section of pattern to cut 2 upper panels from a heavy-weight fabric (here, gold damask), and bottom section of pattern to cut 2 lower panels from a contrasting heavy-weight fabric (here, gray print).

3 For outside of bag, sew each upper panel to a lower panel; press seam allowances downward. Fuse batting to wrong side and cut to same size. Quilt, letting fabric design (such as stripe of gold damask) determine quilting design. Pin Star block on one side (front), centering between sides and overlapping lower panel. Stitch in the ditch along

piping around sides and bottom of Star block. Stitch around again to ensure durability for this large pocket. If desired, add a patch pocket to back of the bag.

4 For an interior pocket, pin two matching pieces of fabric together with right sides facing. Stitch along top edge, and turn right sides out. Press, and turn top edge down 2½"; topstitch to hem. Place this piece between the 2 lining pieces, with right sides facing and bottom edges even. Stitch along sides and bottom. Clip bottom corners and press seam allowances open. To "box" the bottom so bag can stand up, line up end of bottom seam with adjacent side seam. Measure 2" from the triangle peak that's formed, and mark the base of the triangle. See photo w. Stitch along base of triangle and then again, 1/8" away, to reinforce seam. Trim away the triangle, 1/4" beyond stitched triangle base.

5 Place bag exterior front and back together with right sides facing. Stitch around sides and bottom. For extra strength, stitch along same seam line again. Clip bottom corners and press seam allowances open. Box the bottom as in previous step (x).

6 Pin open top edge of bag exterior 2" to wrong side. To hold crossbar of handles, measure them and cut 2 pieces of grosgrain ribbon 1" longer. Turn cut edges ¼" to one side twice and topstitch. Fold each lengthwise in half, right side out, and pin along center of bag front and back, as shown (y).

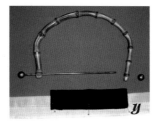

Baste in place. Turn rim of lining 2½" to wrong side. Slip lining inside bag exterior, aligning side seams, and pin lining in place ½" from top edge. Working from the exterior, topstitch around, ¼" from the top.

7 Add a magnet or frog (Chinese knot and loop) closure wherever you want them. Embellish crazy star center with buttons and/or charms. ●

playbook

Top row, left to right:
Based on a Nine-Patch but with a slightly larger center, this classic Star block is also known as Variable Star, Evening Star, Ohio Star, and by many other names. Keep the same grid, but instead of drawing star points from midpoints of the center square, shift the starting points.

Middle row:
Go wild and skew the grid. Start the star points at the midpoints, or move them as suggested by the red dots on the far right.

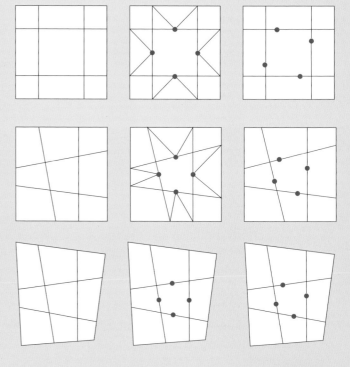

Bottom row, directly above:
Go wilder and don't limit the block to a square. Try a quadrangle like the ones here or the one at left, enlarged as you wish. Or, make a wonky star of your own and then outline it to define the block. Glow wild!

quiltmaking basics

Be wild, not "be-wildered!" Look over this section before you begin a project. And if you ever feel you are in unfamiliar territory, refer to the info here to put you back on the path to successful quiltmaking.

material matters

As we all know, fabrics are the primary element in any quilted project and so they are listed first on every "what you'll need" list in this book. While some designs feature a heavy-weight decorator fabric, and the Star bag boasts a selection of fancy fashion fabrics, most of the designs call for 100% cotton, medium-weight fabric. Yardage amounts are based on 42" widths. When possible, the how-to's suggest using fat quarters (18" x 21") or fat eighths (9" x 21"). Pre-wash all cottons with hot water, and dry in the dryer to shrink fabrics and remove excess dyes (avoiding unpleasant surprises after you've invested a lot of time and effort!). Remove the selvages—the tightly woven, lengthwise edges of the yardage.

- Thread snips or small embroidery scissors
- Pins and a pincushion
- Sewing needle
- Fabric pencils in light and dark colors
- Seam ripper for "oops" moments, and tweezers for pulling out threads
- Steam iron, ironing surface, and non-stick presser sheet

supplies strategy

Though not usually mentioned in the "what you'll need" lists, these staples are essential, so make sure you have them on hand:

- Paper, tracing paper, and freezer paper, for patterns
- Pencils, pencil sharpeners
- Fine-tip permanent markers
- Graph paper, pencil, ruler, and colored pencils, for design play
- Scissors for paper and fabric
- Rotary cutting supplies: 45mm rotary cutter with a sharp blade, acrylic rulers, cutting mat
- Sewing machine in good working order, with the following presser feet: ¼" patchwork foot, open toe foot, zipper foot, darning foot for free motion (open or clear)

piece and understanding

OK friends, this is not the place for going wild. Patience, restraint, and consistency yield the best results. Unless otherwise indicated, place pieces together with right sides facing and edges even. Pin when useful to align edges and match corners; remove pins as you machine-stitch and do not stitch over them. Leave ¼" seam allowances, as uniformly as you possibly can.

BOUNCE IDEAS OFF A WALL—
a design wall

The painter stands back from the easel to assess the composition-in-progress. And she walks away, for a coffee break or a good night's sleep, to approach the piece with a fresh perspective. So, too, anyone who pursues quiltmaking (with anything other than a fully-prescribed kit with a fabric pack) needs to stand back and judge how fabric choices work together. Are color combos-contrasting or blending? If I squint, are there still clear value differences? Will a zinger or accent add life? Do the prints and patterns in the fabric complement each other, or are the visual textures too close and monotonous? Is there a focal point? Does one fabric stick out too much? Have I arranged the blocks so the colors are balanced? And the ultimate questions: Do I like what I see? Is it the best it can be?

You cannot answer these design questions by viewing your work on a table surface. It's just too close! The best tool to add to your quilting arsenal is a design wall. On this large vertical surface, you can arrange your blocks and stand back about 6 feet to consider your arrangement. You can leave things up during a break that's minutes short or days-long, so you can come back to the project with fresh eyes. The ideal design wall is minimally 8 feet high and 4 feet wide and can be easily made. Get foam core board from the lumberyard, and stretch white or neutral-colored flannel over it, stapling and duct-taping to make it taut. Attach permanently to a wall. Or, just let it lean in place; when not in use, store it behind a door or freestanding cabinet. Patches will usually "stick" to the flannel surface on their own and larger border or background pieces can be pinned in place. All of the pieces can be moved around and rearranged as you assess and reassess...until the design works for you.

Lack the space or time to set up a design wall? Try a temporary alternative: Tape a large piece of batting or felt to a wall. Or, hang a flannel backed vinyl tablecloth flannel-side out over a door or curtain rod.

Can't stand back far enough? Look at each phase of the composition in any of 3 ways:

*   Through the large end of a pair of binoculars
*   Through a reducing glass, available at art stores and quilt shops
*   With a photo. Take a picture with your digital camera and look at the image on camera, and printed out. While you're at it, convert the image to black and white. Any kiosk at a photo center has this option, which will ensure that your piece has a good mix of light, medium, and dark tones. Consider all the possibilities, and use the images to help steer you to a great design.

Now you're ready to sew the patches together and assemble your quilt project, confident that it's going to be well worth the time and effort.

pressing issues

When piecing, try to press as you go. You can, however, get away with finger-pressing seams until you finish a unit, or make a lot of units, and then do all the pressing with an iron. Use a hot, dry iron set for cotton, or the setting appropriate for the most temperamental fabric you are using. Never iron directly on metallics, synthetics, or fancy fabrics; use a non-stick presser cloth as a "go-between."

there's an app for that:
fusible appliqué

"Fusible web" is a thin sheet that, when pressed to the back of fabric, allows the fabric to adhere to another surface. The heat of the iron melts the web, which then acts like glue. It's also a sealant, leaving edges that hardly ravel at all. Some types of fusible web have a release paper; others do not. Web comes in various weights and each brand is different, so follow the manufacturer's instructions for the fusible web you are using and consult your quilt shop, if necessary, for recommendations as to which weight and type will work best for the project you are doing.

Protect your iron and ironing surface from the web adhesive with a pressing cloth, nonstick pressing sheet, or piece of release paper. For those inevitable "Oh no!" moments when you do gunk up your iron with fusible glue, be prepared to rub the sole plate on folded scrap fabric, a used dryer sheet, or release paper. For heavier clean-ups, squeeze a dab of hot iron cleaner onto a wad of scrap fabric and rub the iron over the fabric.

Fused fabric is almost never permanently bonded. Machine-appliqué, topstitching, or quilting will keep appliqués from lifting over time—and add a dynamic design element. Use a heavier thread in the needle, such as a 30 or 40-weight or even a 12 topstitching thread. Go wild with shiny or variegated threads. But always pre-test your machine's tension, as the fusible makes fabrics stiffer than usual.

quilt to the hilt

First, make a quilt sandwich: Cut batting and backing fabric a little larger all around than the quilt top. If you are not using fusible batting, make giant basting stitches (see photo below), or insert safety pins or straight pins to keep the layers from shifting.

Make a scrap sandwich of the same or similar fabrics, so you can test and alter the tension on your sewing machine every time you choose a different thread. Ideally, start quilting in the center and work outward in all directions.

Consider quilting in the ditch—right along the seam, to flatten the seam and make the patch or unit of patches stand out. Or, choose the simplest quilting patterns that will complement your piecing but save you the hassles of measuring, marking, or stenciling. A freehand grid in variegated thread makes a design stronger and more cohesive.

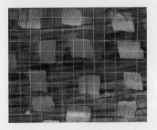

Stripes in the fabric or masking tape pressed in place can guide you in quilting even lines. Or, use the width of the presser foot or markings on the bed of the sewing machine to space out the quilting lines evenly. Want curvy lines? Keep them gentle, or choose deep scallops, swirls, and curls in free-motion quilting.

For free-motion quilting, use a darning foot, which allows you to move the quilt sandwich in any direction. Practice, practice, practice...on a test piece that's similar in thickness to your project.

Unless your sewing machine has a stitch regulator, you just have to get used to simultaneously moving the piece and running the machine smoothly and consistently. Work freehand, meandering over the surface to fill the space with a simple pattern. Check out these examples:

- Follow the print

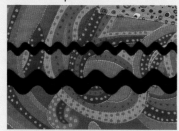

- Mimic the piecing

- One big spiral

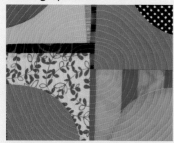

- Complement angles with curves

hang-ups? sew what!

Will your creation hang on a wall? If so, create a sleeve or channel casing for a dowel or rod. Cut a rectangle of fabric 3" shorter than the top edge of the quilt, and 4½" wide. Hem the short ends of the rectangle, fold it lengthwise in half, and lightly press. Center it along the top edge of the backing, with raw edges even. As you bind your quilt, these raw edges will be enclosed. After the binding is attached, slip-stitch along the bottom folded edge of the casing to secure it to the backing. Insert a slat or dowel, with holes or eye-hooks at each end.

binding action

If a project in this book calls for binding, make it a nice, firm, double-fold binding. Cut 2½"-wide strips along the grain, and piece the strips with diagonal seams, until you've got a piece 10" longer than the perimeter of the quilt. Press the strip in half lengthwise, with the right side facing out.

Unless otherwise indicated, start at the bottom of the quilt, a few inches from a corner, and leave a 5" tail. Pin the raw edges even with the quilt top. Stitch the binding to the quilt, leaving ¼" seam allowances and removing pins as you come to them. See photo a. To miter the corner, stop stitching ¼" from a corner, and take a backstitch. Remove the quilt from under the presser foot (b). Fold the binding up so it's

flush with the adjacent edge (photo c). Fold it down again, alongside the new edge (photo d). Insert the needle ¼" from both sides, take a couple of stitches, backstitch, and then continue on down that side (e).

When you approach the place where you began, overlap the folded starting end, and trim the finishing end of the binding at a 45° angle. Finish sewing the binding to the quilt.

Bring the long folded edge of the binding over the edges of the quilt sandwich, and pin it to the backing. At each corner, fold one side in neatly, then the other, pinning to hold. See photos f and g. Use thread in a color that matches the binding, and slip-stitch along the fold to cover the machine stitching.

let's face it!

This edge finish has long been used to neatly tailor necklines and armholes. More and more art quilters routinely forego the thin line of demarcation that frames and reins in the design as a binding does. By using a facing instead, the eye can imagine that the design continues off beyond the edges...

To make a facing, cut a 2½"-wide strip along the straight of grain, 1" longer than each edge you are facing. Begin with the bottom edge. Press one long edge of the corresponding facing strip ¼" to wrong side. Place the unpressed edge along the raw edge of the quilt with right sides facing. Stitch ¼" from the edges. See photo h. Fold the facing all the way over to the backing; don't let any of the facing show on the front. Press the seam and edges firmly. Trim the ends of the facing even with the quilt edges. Use fusible web tape to secure the facing to the backing; see photo i. Or, pin, then slip-stitch the folded edges of the facing to the backing of the quilt. Repeat to apply a facing to the top edge—unless you are adding a sleeve for hanging. (If that is the case, plan for a large overhang at the top, or bind this edge.)

Next, pin facing strips to the long sides, folding ends under ½". Sew along the facing, ¼" from the raw edges, turn, press, and secure the folded edge as before. Slip-stitch along the ends as well.

label it yours!

With the possible exception of a potholder, your project isn't done 'til it tells your name and when you made it. Why not...

• Make an extra quilt block, and mark pertinent info on the patch. Pin and stitch to the back, covering the raw edges with hand-couched ribbon.

• Document your work: Start by pressing fusible web to the wrong side of light-colored fabric, which acts as a stabilizer as well as a fusible. With the release paper still in place on the back, use a fabric pen to do some journaling on the fabric. Press with a hot, dry iron to heat-set the ink. Then peel off the release paper, and cut out the label with pinking shears...maybe in a crazy quadrangular shape! Fuse it to the back of your project.

• Free-motion quilt your name and date on the front of your work, like a painter does at the bottom of a finished canvas.

meet the quilt designers

Eleanor Levie recently moved with her hubby to Center City, Philadelphia, and found downsizing the perfect excuse to give away all her mauve fabrics and ditsy prints. Author, editor, and book producer, she's the creative force behind *Unforgettable TOTE BAGS*, two *Skinny Quilts & Table Runners* books, 8 volumes of the Rodale's Successful Quilting Library series, *American Quiltmaking: 1970-2000*, *Great Little Quilts*, and many other quilt books. Elly enjoys putting fancy fashion fabrics, sun prints, foil-lined coffee and tea bags, and other unexpected materials into her quilts and wearables. Even more, she loves sharing her unusual vintage quilt collection, and inspiring quilters to push the envelope and go wild! Visit her at EleanorLevie.com, and send her pictures of *your* wild new quilt blocks!

Karla Alexander lives in beautiful Salem, Oregon with her husband, the youngest of their sons, and Lucy the dog. She is the innovative quilt designer who taught us how to cut, shuffle, and play in books such as *Stack the Deck!*, *Stack a New Deck!*, and *Stack the Deck Revisited*. Traditional blocks are routinely the springboards for Karla's new blocks, which allow for lots of fabrics in surprising combinations. Highly prolific, she has made hundreds of quilts, with hundreds more waiting to be made. In great demand at workshops and quilt retreats, she has taught thousands of students how to quilt using a variety of methods in addition to her own. Besides creating quilts for books and patterns, Karla designs rulers for Creative Grids Rulers. Check out all her books and patterns at saginawstreetquilts.com.

Pamela Goecke Dinndorf of central Minnesota designs uncommonly simple but simply spectacular patterns under the title Aardvark quilts. Such wildlife is hardly to be found on her local scene, but a brainstorming session with her husband led her to choose a company name with two As that would appear at the top of the alphabetical listings in quilting directories of vendors and designers. The quirky name turns out to be as memorable as her quilt designs. An obsession with the magical effects of color has taken Pam on a career path through fashion and interior design before coming to quilt design. She revels in combining powerful colors and prints in dynamic concoctions. Her designs appear in many quilting magazines and books, with a book of her own in the works. Her patterns are available at, where else?– aardvarkquilts.com.

Malka Dubrawsky of Austin, Texas was inspired in an eighth grade art class and graduated from college with a Bachelor of Fine Arts in Studio Art. Being at home with children pushed her into working with textiles, and the quilt world is the better for it. Malka has worked primarily as a fiber artist for several years now and counts herself lucky to be included in some prestigious shows and publications such as QuiltNational and Visions and Fiberarts: Design Book 7. Luck had nothing to do with it, as you can see from her books, *Color Your Cloth: A Quilter's Guide to Dyeing and Patterning Fabric* and *Fresh Quilting: Fearless, Color, Design, and Inspiration.* She keeps very busy teaching and making quilted pieces from her own hand-dyed and patterned fabric. Drool over her stuff on etsy: stitchindye.etsy.com, and find out more at stitchindye.blogspot.com.

Tonya Ricucci of southern Florida is passionate about quilts that make the Quilt Police cry. Thanks to Gwen Marston's book, *Liberated Quiltmaking,* Tonya enjoys piecing without measuring. She recently authored *Word Play Quilts,* to share her free-pieced letter techniques. Crumbs and strings (leftover fabric bits and strips), houses and fans, and Halloween-y themes can also be found in her work. Despite an imprecise and whimsical style of piecing, she is an avid hand quilter. Besides Gwen Marston, Tonya loves Roberta Horton, Amish quilts, the work of Anna Williams and the quilters of Gees Bend. Oh, and English Breakfast tea and TiVO and sci-fi and her husband and four cats. Find out what else tickles her fancy at unrulyquilter.com or lazygalquilting.blogspot.com.

Elizabeth Rosenberg lives in White Plains, part of the Greater NYC megalopolis, with her husband and her little chihuahua, Topolina (the same name Italians use for Minnie Mouse). She puts her talents and sewing machine to work creating art from fabric and thread. But much of her time these days is spent at college, where she has returned after a more than thirty-year break to raise two sons and run her own quilt pattern company. She is currently a full-time student for a degree program in the arts. When she can, she teaches and lectures about art quilting, such as the Goddess Project. Her latest award-winning pieces and quilt quild presentations feature abstract images of the flowing line, which is also the subject of her upcoming quilt book. Go to elizabethrosenberg.com (be sure to click on her portfolio).

resources

Ask for products featured in this book at your local retail stores, or contact the manufacturer for more information.

Batting:
Fusiboo fusible bamboo/cotton batting from Fairfield Processing, consumer@fairfieldworld.com, 800-980-8000

Nature-Fil Blend Quilt Batting, bamboo/cotton from Fairfield Processing (see above)

Quilter's 80/20 batting for hand-quilted pillow, from Fairfield Processing (see above)

Thermal batting for potholders: Insul-Bright polyester batting needle-punched to Mylar, in 22" and 45" widths, from Warm and Natural, warmcompany.com

Buttons:
Favorite Findings Big Basic Buttons by B. Blumenthal, 1¼" in diameter, color: Carnival, 6 per package, blumenthallansing.com

Fabrics:
Collections from Kaffe Fassett and Brandon Mably featured in Log Cabin Split Level: gloriouscolor.com

Gray print decorator fabric featured in Star, Partly Crazy bag: Ikea Stockholm Blad in gray, ikea.com

Fusible interfacing and web:
Peltex-II, 2-sided fusible ultra firm stabilizer, 20"-wide from Pellon, pellonideas.com, 727-388-7171

Wonder-Under Fusible web with paper backing from Pellon (see above)

Pillow forms:
Bamboo Pillow Inserts, 18" square, used in Rail Fence Derailed pillows, bamboo blend with 100% cotton cover, from Fairfield Processing (see above)

Feather-fil Pillow Inserts, 20" square, used in Drunkards Off the Path pillows, 95% feather and 5% down filling with 100% cotton cover, from Fairfield Processing (see above)

Purse handles:
Set of 2 interchangeable half moon shapes with metal rod, 6¾" wide x 5" high, Tall Poppy Craft Supplies, tallpoppycraft.com, 212-813-3223

acknowledgments

 Thank you, Cheryl Johnson at Leisure Arts, who paid me the tremendous compliment of seeking me out and offering me this assignment. You have been an unflagging source of support.

Hugs & kisses to hub Carl Harrington—espouser of risk-taking, and son Sam—advocate for adventure. When do I get to stay home and relax?

Kudos, phenomenal photographer Donna H. Chiarelli. You make shots that surpass all expectations, and shoots much more fun than they oughta be.

Total awe for the keen eye and insanely fresh point of view of Diane Pizzuto, freelance graphic designer. Pzzt: You wowed me when you answered my craigslist ad, and you never stopped wowing me.

You rock, Valerie L. Egar, and I could not have produced such clear, reliable, and lively copy without you to critique every word and kick it all up several notches.

Being able to draw on your keen mastery of Adobe Illustrator, Rachel Shelburne, is what assures me that this book will reflect professionalism throughout the line art.

Luxe Home Philadelphia (luxehomepa.com), one of my favorite sources of urban chic, has my gratitude for availing us of such an exquisite location for photography.

Fairfield Processing Corp., aka Fairfield World: thanks for supplying the wonderful batting and pillow forms.

Eternal indebtedness to the quilting stars, Elizabeth, Karla, Malka, Pam, and Tonya. You generously shared your time and talents, and gave me designs beyond my wildest dreams.